PRAISE FOR
EXPLAINING A DRESS

"Here is a sensory plunge at once harsh and kind, historic and immediate, factual and emotional, heart-rending yet courage-making. Brava! for this remarkable art of erasure and indeed vindication."
> —**Diana Tokaji,** 2024 (Not in Love) Tanka Challenge First Place Winner, and author of *Six Women in a Cell*, which won Best Indie Book Award Nonfiction 2021

"*Explaining a Dress* offers a chorus, a constellation of voices and lives tragically damaged or, worse, ended. This collection of found poems curated into erasure form reminds us of what is left unsaid and, more importantly, what requires timely and timeless shouting."
> —**Rebecca Evans,** author of *Safe Handling* and *Tangled by Blood*

"Using the form of erasure, the poet introduces us to a chorus of trans-feminine people erased from history. Erasure is always an act of oppression. But in using erasure as a poetic technique the collection becomes a powerful historical reckoning that is complex and poignant and serves as both a tribute to and a vindication of the lives erased."
> —**Nancy Miller Gomez,** author of *Inconsolable Objects*

"What a brilliant idea *Explaining a Dress* is. A poetry collection that highlights the struggles of trans women in a series of erased newspaper articles dating between 1889 and 1959.

"[*Explaining a Dress*] challenges the reader, prods at the brain cells with a red-hot poker, stirring up feelings of indignation and injustice, and then forces us to lay back in our lazy boy chairs to contemplate how far we have come, what exactly lies ahead, and has our journey been in vain?"
> —**Yasmin Goldie,** Frontier Poetry Editorial Team Member

EXPLAINING
A DRESS

TRANSFEMININE ERASURE
AND VINDICATION

JESSIE KEARY

RED MARE
PRESS

Edited by Madeline McConico.

Cover design by Emelie Mano.

Interior design by Julianne Johnson.

RED MARE
PRESS

Red Mare Press / Discover New Art, LLC

70 SW Century Drive, Suite 100442, Bend, Oregon 97702

www.redmarepress.com

Red Mare Press is a division of Discover New Art, LLC.

The Red Mare Press name and logo are trademarks of Discover New Art, LLC.

The publisher is not responsible for websites (or their content) that are not owned by the publisher.

ISBN 979-8-9901838-7-2

Printed in the United States of America.

*In honor of the gender-expansive people
who have always existed and always will*

"I defy any doctor in the world to prove that I am not a woman. I have lived, dressed, acted just what I am — a woman.

It's only petty maliciousness that is trying to cause me heartache and harm. If they would devote the same amount of energy to local problems that are hurting the community, it would be much better. I have lived a good life and a Christian life. And though I am a Christian, I revere all religious faiths. I have lived, a good citizen, for many years in this town and am going to die a good citizen, but I am going to die a woman."

— Lucy Hale,
at her perjury trial, answering
the charge of masquerading
Ventura, CA 1945

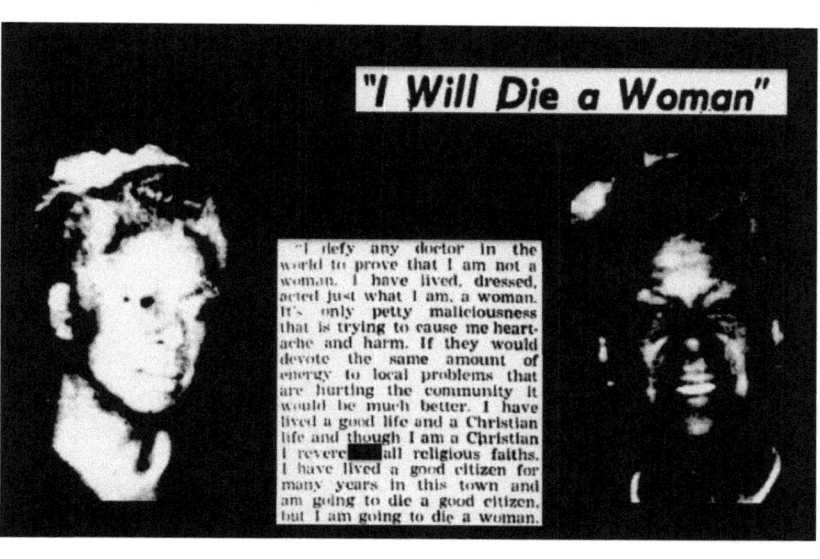

"I Will Die a Woman"

"I defy any doctor in the world to prove that I am not a woman. I have lived, dressed, acted just what I am, a woman. It's only petty maliciousness that is trying to cause me heartache and harm. If they would devote the same amount of energy to local problems that are hurting the community it would be much better. I have lived a good life and a Christian life and though I am a Christian I revere all religious faiths. I have lived a good citizen for many years in this town and am going to die a good citizen, but I am going to die a woman.

C●NTENTS

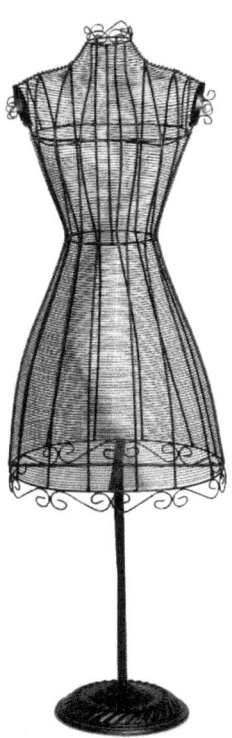

ELUDING

Massillon, OH 1951

A woman dodged three police bullets
shortly after midnight Monday.

She   was tall with a slender build,

          wore a long dress and white scarf.

She was strange to those around her,
so they cruised the area for her blood.

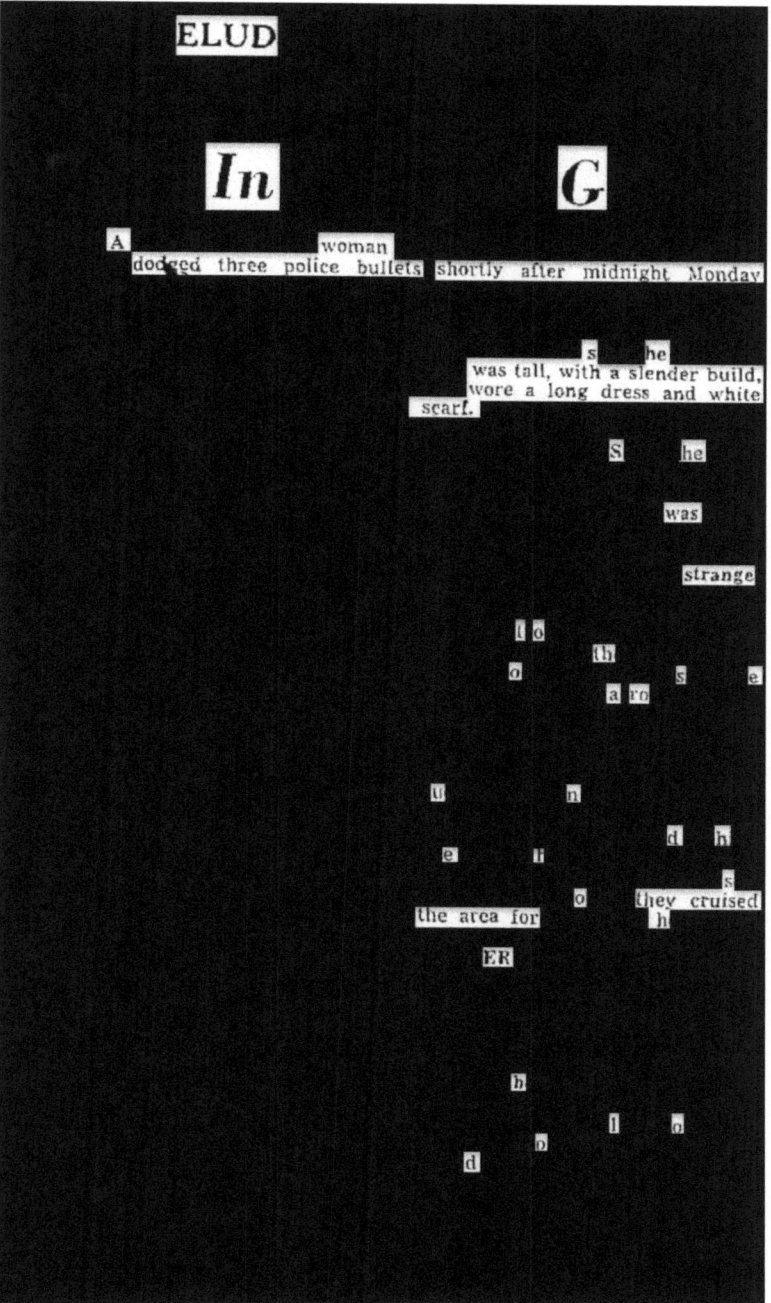

ELUD

In   *G*

A   woman
dodged three police bullets shortly after midnight Monday

                                    s   he
                        was tall, with a slender build,
                        wore a long dress and white
                scarf.

                                    S   he

                                    was

                                    strange

                    t o
                    o   th   s   e
                                a re

            u   n

        e   li   d   h
                                            s
        the area for   o   they cruised
                            ER   h

                        b

                    o   l   o
        d

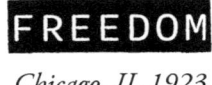

Chicago, IL 1923

She told the story
of a dual life —

a boy in Chillicothe,
a woman in Chicago.

"I was naturally
a very quiet child.

I wore boy's clothing,
but I always wanted

to wear a woman's clothes
because I felt easier."

FREEDOM

"I was naturally a very quiet child ▮▮▮▮▮ I wore boy's clothing, but I always wanted to wear a woman's clothes because I felt easier."

he told the story of a dual life boy in Chillicothe woman in Chicago

MASQUERADING

Honolulu, HI 1920

Benita with   the marriage certificate,

the wedding ring,

a gingham gown,

high-heeled slippers,

long, curly hair,

earrings with pendants.

She is   25 years old.

She will be given   a haircut,

a man's clothes.

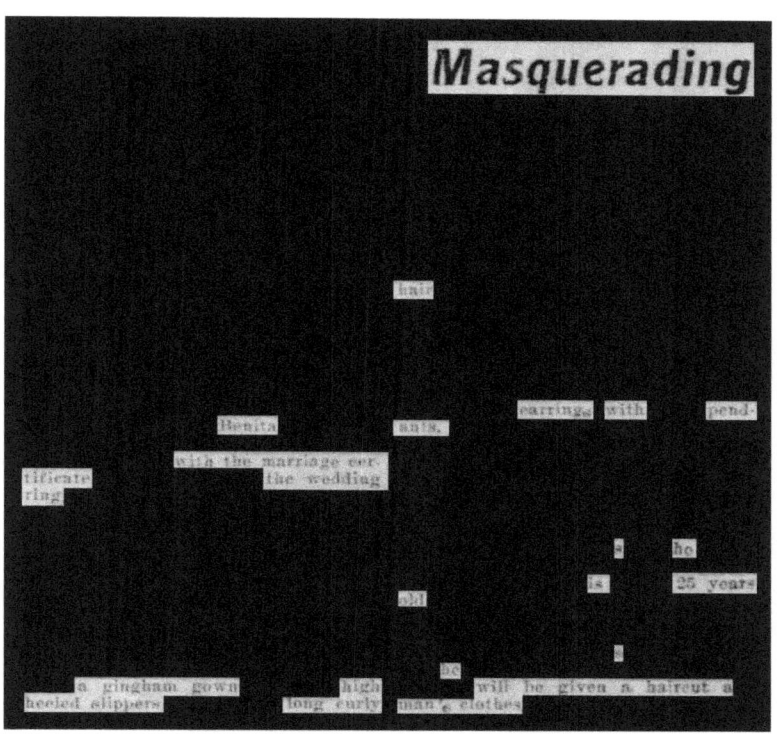

NATURE'S FREAK

New York City, NY 1896

Man is a freak for
punishing   softness,
                 grace,
                 goodness.

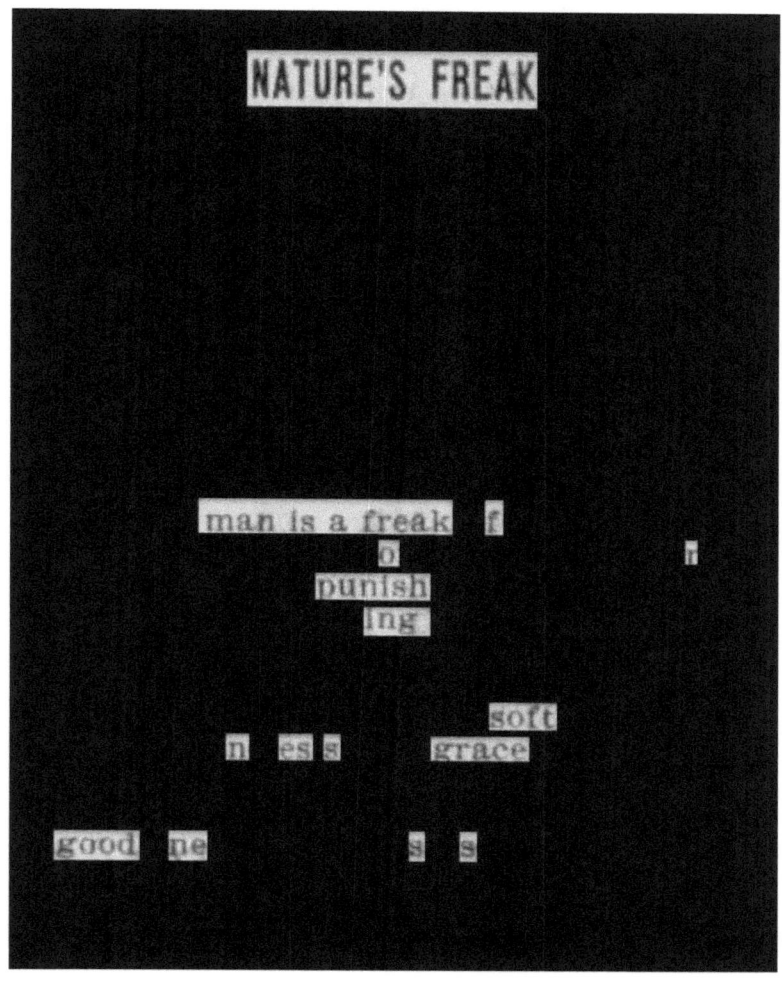

SENT TO THE ARMY

Clovis, NM 1943

All female attire sold, she will
invest the money in war bonds.
She has been a woman for eight
years and worked as a bar maid
in many cities. Her home is
Blossom, Texas — left in 1935
and never been back.

> "I started as a girl
> in my school days.
>
> It was embarrassing, and
> my schoolmates kidded
> me for a sissy.
>
> I suppose this led to
> my leading the life
> of a woman."

When taken before the secretary
of the draft board, she insisted on
being registered under the name:

> "Sondra."

sent to the army
all   female attire
sold,   s   he   will
invest the money in war bonds.
s   h
e

has been
a woman for eight years
and   worked as a bar maid
in many cities   he
r
home is Blossom, Texas.   left
in 1935 and   never been
back.
"I started   as a
girl   in my school days.

It was embarrassing and my
school mates kidded   me for a
sissy. I suppose this led to my
leading the life of a woman

When   taken before
the secretary of the draft board
S   he insisted on being reg-
istered under the name   Sondra

A WOMAN

St. Louis, MO 1929

The body of
a woman found
inhaling a secret
learned living
is one attempt
to communicate.

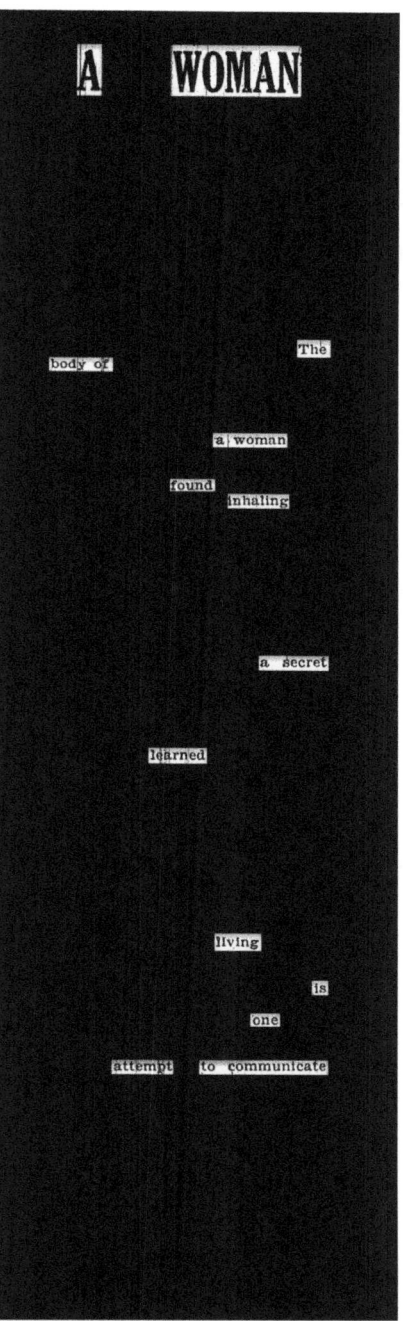

LENA

Bridgeport, CT 1915

A woman, so perfectly made up,

passed upon the streets of Bridgeport.

She worked with several hundred girls.

She was   adept with the use of

                   liquid rouge,

                   a model of artistic beauty,

                   the envy of every woman,

        with   the finest

                   white silk shirts,

                   lingerie, tailored

                   broadcloth suits,

                   and fancy light

                   ball dresses

                                 in her room.

She was hanging a picture when

contour of calf,

actions at ease,

timbre of voice   led to discovery,

no charges —

        no statute prevents

        masquerading   in the house.

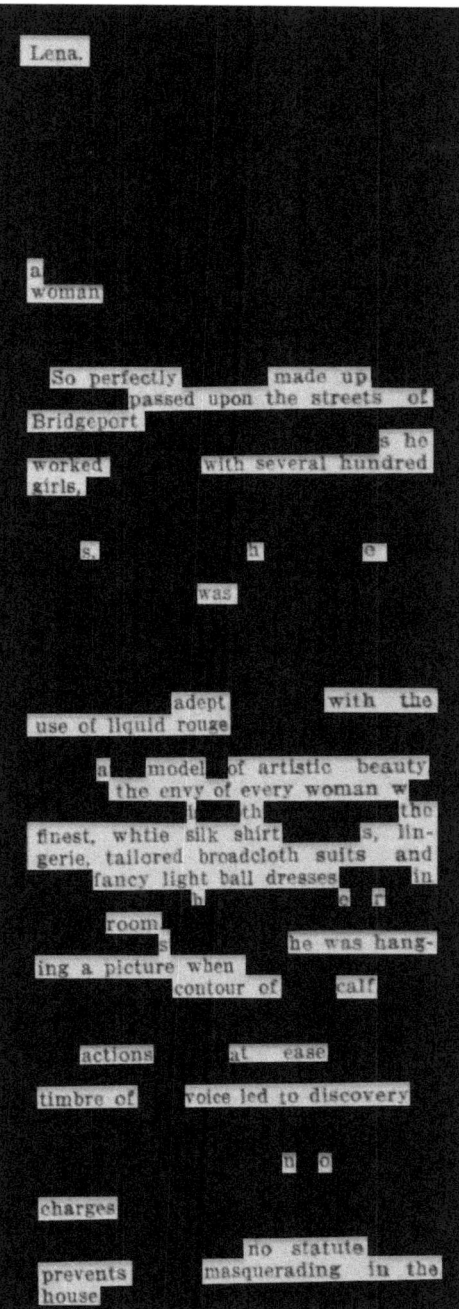

Lena,

a
woman

So perfectly   made up
          passed upon the streets of
Bridgeport
                              s he
worked   with several hundred
girls,

      s,   h   e

          was

          adept   with the
use of liquid rouge

a   model of artistic beauty
    the envy of every woman w
i   th   the
finest, whtie silk shirt   s, lin-
gerie, tailored broadcloth suits and
    fancy light ball dresses   in
      h   e   r
    room
      s   he was hang-
ing a picture when
          contour of   calf

    actions   at   ease

timbre of   voice led to discovery

              n o

charges

          no statute
prevents   masquerading in the
house

SLAIN

New York City, NY 1937

Life is   bare legs tied with a bed sheet,

a disordered apartment,

a head badly battered,

a bent metal pitcher,

hearing a struggle,

explaining a dress.

SLAIN

life-
is bare legs
tied with a bed sheet,

a   disordered
apartment

a
head badly battered   a bent
metal   pitcher

hear-
ing a struggle,

ex-
plaining   a
dress

AUNTIE RACHAEL

Columbia, SC 1930

a familiar figure

a woman in demand

a nurse

a prisoner

for wearing dresses

since   a child

no charge of misconduct

of any sort (other than that)

AUNTIE

Ra-
chael
a
familiar figure
a woman
in demand
a purse
a
prisoner

for

wearing dresses since a child

no charge
of misconduct of any sort, other
than that

A SOCIETY FAVORITE

Belle Fourche, SD 1907

A belle has light within,
setting the pace for society,
breaking hearts until they

break her. Helen disappeared
once old admirers saw her
dresses as disguises.

a Society Favorite

a

Belle   has
    light   w   l
        t   hi
        n   setting
the pace for society

            breaking   hearts
        un   t
        i   the   v   B
                        r   ea
                                  k
H   er
        Helen

            disappeared
                    o
n   ce
                        old
        admirers   w
s a
            he
    r
d   re   s   s   e
    s   a   s

    D   l   s
        g   u
la   e   s

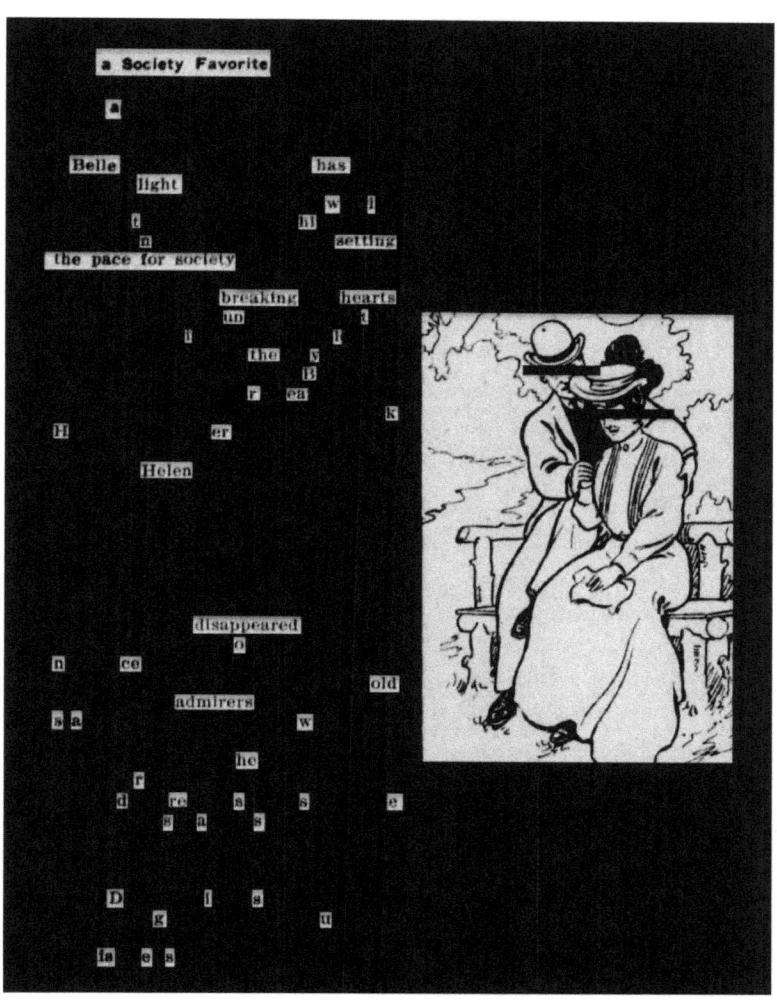

CHRISTINE

Massapequa, NY 1959

I sometimes wonder, if I had been born
average — I won't say normal — what
would I have been like? It's fruitless.
If I had to go through it all again, I
wouldn't do anything differently.

I had dinner with a fellow I went to
high school with. I asked him if I had
changed. Everybody at the table laughed,
but. He said, 'No. You haven't changed,
and I like you a lot better this way.'

Of course, people come to see me because
they're curious about me. Well, if I weren't
me, I'd be curious about me, too. But a lot of
people come back to see me, and that's only
because they like me. It's more of an honor

than I can say. I don't know that I always
wanted to be in show business, but. When
you think about it, where else could I go?
The older I grow, the more I learn.

I once thought I had no way to solve my
problems and better keep them to myself.

I was wrong. That's what makes
a tragedy out of life.

Christine

."I sometimes wonder,"
  "if I had been born average
—I won't say normal — what
would I have been like? It's
fruitless
            if I had to go through
all of it again. I wouldn't do any-
thing differently."

"Of course people   come to
see me because they're curious
about me. Well, if I weren't me,
I'd be curious about me, too.
But a lot of people come back
to see me   And that's only
because they like me. It's more
of an honor than I can say.
"I don't know that I always
wanted to be in show business.
But when you think about it,
where else could I go?"

That's what makes a tragedy
out of a life.

"The older I grow,"
  "the more I learn

                 I once
thought I had no way to solve
my problems and   better
keep them to myself.
       I was wrong

"I had dinner with a fellow
I went to high school with,"
       I asked him if I had
changed   Ev-
erybody at the table laughed,
but he said: 'No. You haven't
changed. And I like you a lot
better this way.' "

IN TROUBLE AGAIN

Enid, OK 1908

A feminine voice is fortune.
Enjoy notoriety because of it.

If taken (locked up),
own your feminine
consciousness —

remarkable,

worthy.

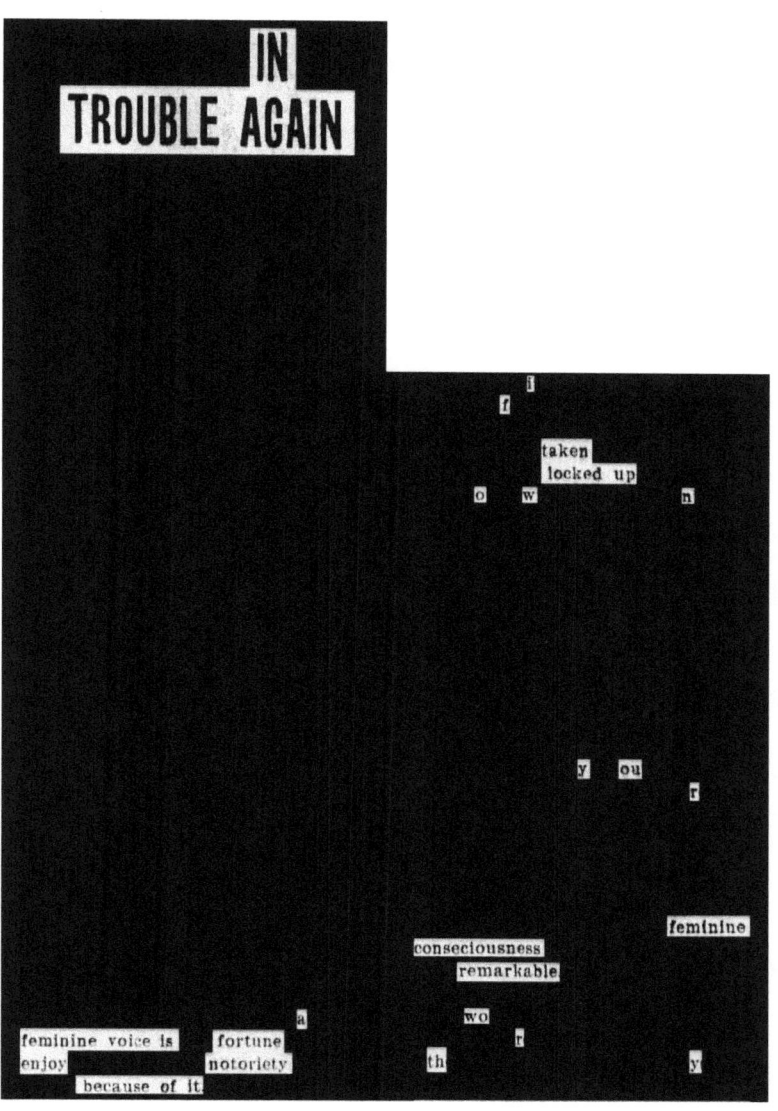

PETTICOATS

Montgomery, AL 1889

A society leader,
bustle and all,
was run in by police,
suspecting her secret.

Mary Jenny waltzed
up to the station
and stated the "disguise"
had been assumed because

she could get along better
in this weary world.

She had been galivanting
around Montgomery
without being suspected.

She had been herself —
belle of balls, leader
of swell social affairs.

The police think she's
concealing something
of a criminal nature.

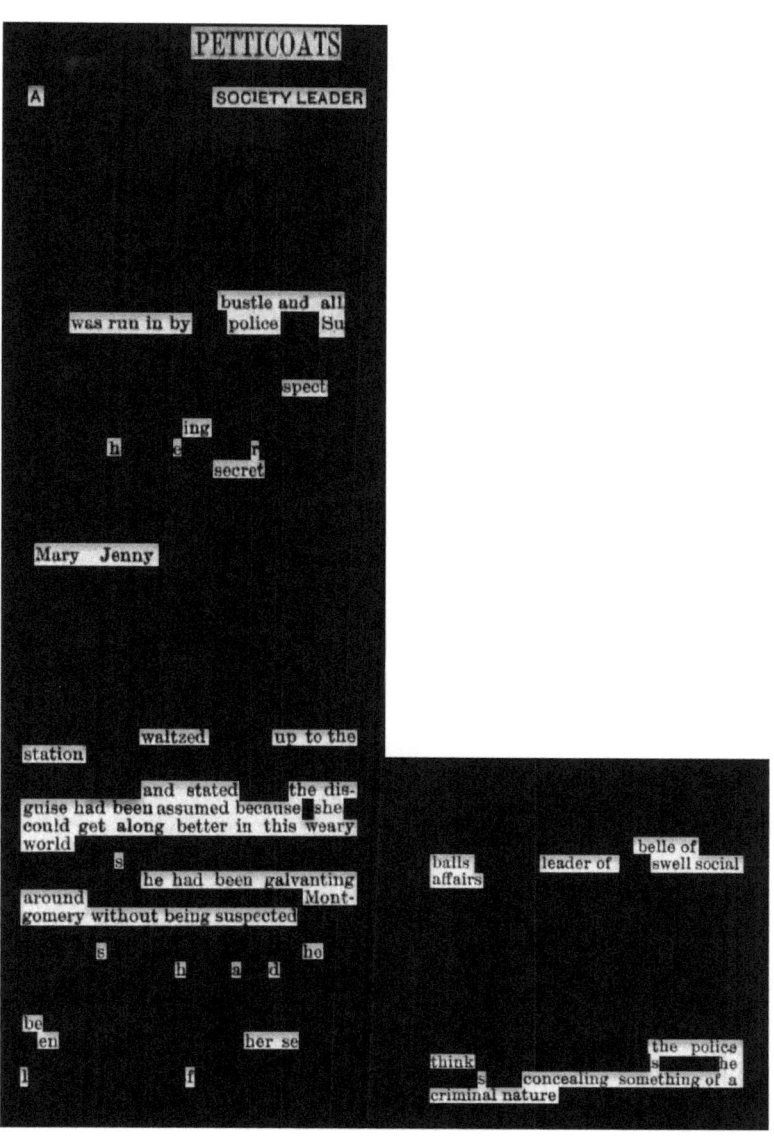

PETTICOATS

A   SOCIETY LEADER

bustle and all
was run in by   police   Su

spect

ing
h   secret

Mary   Jenny

waltzed   up to the
station
and stated   the dis-
guise had been assumed because she
could get along better in this weary
world
s
he had been galvanting
around   Mont-
gomery without being suspected

s   ho
h   a   d

be
en   her se
l   f

balls   leader of   belle of
affairs   swell social

think   the police
s   he
s   concealing something of a
criminal nature

WOMAN CUTS SELF

Gettysburg, PA 1956

a throat a pocketknife two a.m. sitting at the bar

sitting at the bar two a.m. a pocketknife a throat

a throat a pocketknife two a.m. sitting at the bar

sitting at the bar two a.m. a pocketknife a throat

a throat a pocketknife two a.m. sitting at the bar

sitting at the bar two a.m. a pocketknife a throat

WOMAN CUTS SELF

a

throat   a pocketknife

2 a.m.   sitting at the

bar

NOW A BRIDE

Miami, FL 1959

She's a happy newlywed
in a Miami apartment.

Her former identity
came to light in
the Miami Herald.

Charlotte said,
"All I have done is
merely correct a mistake.

It is a tragic social problem.

My psyche has always
been female. I always thought,
felt and reacted like a woman."

Her childhood and the years
before she became a woman
were very unhappy, she said.

"I was miserable, and
I wanted to die."

She said her married life
is normal — "All we ask
is just a chance to be happy."

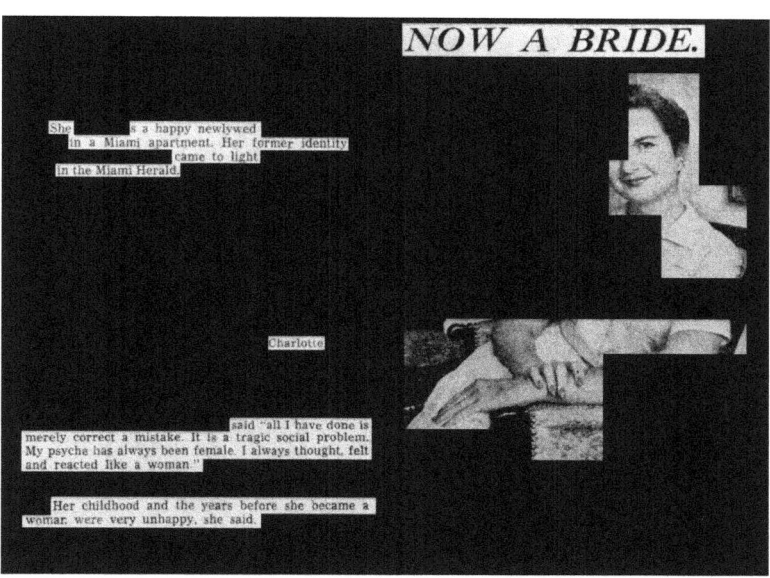

NOW A BRIDE.

She   s a happy newlywed
in a Miami apartment. Her former identity
                came to light
in the Miami Herald.

Charlotte

                        said "all I have done is
merely correct a mistake. It is a tragic social problem.
My psyche has always been female. I always thought, felt
and reacted like a woman."

    Her childhood and the years before she became a
woman were very unhappy, she said.

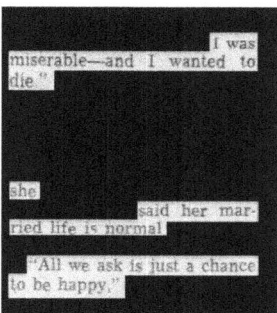

                        I was
miserable—and I wanted to
die."

she
                    said her mar-
ried life is normal

    "All we ask is just a chance
to be happy,"

SOURCE MATERIAL

EPIGRAPH: "Lucy Hicks Says: 'I Will Die a Woman.'" Oxnard Press-Courier, November 5, 1945.

ELUDING: "Patrolman Shoots at Man in Woman's Garb." The Evening Independent (Massillon, OH), July 31, 1951.

FREEDOM: "Girl Bandit Given Freedom, Murder Charge." The Chillicothe Constitution-Tribune, October 5, 1923.

MASQUERADING: "Police Hold Man Masquerading as Woman, Also Male Companion." Honolulu Star-Advertiser, July 28, 1920.

NATURE'S FREAK: "Nature's Freak." The Buffalo News, December 29, 1896.

SENT TO THE ARMY: "Masquerader Is Under Probe of the FBI." Clovis News-Journal, April 5, 1943.

A WOMAN: "Man in Woman's Garb Suicides." Lexington Herald, March 8, 1929.

LENA: "Lena." The Journal (Meriden, CT), March 23, 1915.

SLAIN: "Impersonator Found Slain." Daily Illinois State Journal, May 28, 1937.

AUNTIE RACHAEL: "Man 'Auntie' Falls into Toils of Law." The Gaffney Ledger, June 3, 1930.

A SOCIETY FAVORITE: "Man as Girl Wins Heart of a Lover." The Idaho Recorder, March 7, 1907.

CHRISTINE: "Christine: Her 7 Years as a Woman." The Republic (Columbus, IN), April 11, 1959.

IN TROUBLE AGAIN: "A.J. Baker in Trouble Again." The Iola Daily Record, July 7, 1908.

PETTICOATS: "A Man in Petticoats: A Colored Female Society Leader Turns Out a Man." The Montgomery Advertiser, February 12, 1889.

WOMAN CUTS SELF: "Man Disguised as Woman Cuts Self." New Oxford Item, November 22, 1956.

NOW A BRIDE: "Mr.' Once But Now a Bride." The Kansas City Star, November 14, 1959.

ACKNOWLEDGEMENTS

"Lena" was first published by Palette Poetry as the winner of the 2024 Blackout Poetry Prize.

JESSIE KEARY is a Midwestern, trans writer with too many hobbies. Their poetry can be found in *Transmasculine Poetics* (Sundress Publications), *Sweeter Voices Still* (Belt Publishing), and various corners of the internet.

www.ingramcontent.com/pod-product-compliance
Lightning Source LLC
Chambersburg PA
CBHW051650120626
46551CB00015B/2293